Poems
for Your Soul

Poetry to Uplift your Spirit

CENCA KING

authorHOUSE®

AuthorHouse™
1663 Liberty Drive
Bloomington, IN 47403
www.authorhouse.com
Phone: 833-262-8899

Published by AuthorHouse 11/28/2022

ISBN: 978-1-6655-7646-8 (sc)
ISBN: 978-1-6655-7645-1 (e)

Print information available on the last page.

This book is printed on acid-free paper.

Contents

Still Haven't Arrived

I've come a long way –
But I have a ways to go…
Traveled down some lonely roads –
That I didn't want others to know…
Took part in some foolish things –
Some I wish I'd never done…
Matured in a mighty way –
But I still haven't arrived today…
Made some immoral choices –
That cost me a whole lot…
Agreed to some crazy pledges –
That I wish I could back out of…
Lost a few friendships –
That I wish I had today…
Hurt many a heart –
That didn't deserve the pain…
Ruined a few lives –
That will never be the same…
Deceived by the enemy –
Who played with my mind…
I'm not who I used to be –
But I still haven't arrived…

The Best U Can Be

In life there will be turns –
You will never see coming...
Mountains that need climbing –
That will cost you something...
Some people may mistreat you –
Yet you must forgive...
Following God's examples –
That you have learned over the years...
Storms will arise –
But you must stand the test of time...
Trusting and worshiping God –
Knowing that He is by your side...
Life isn't fair –
So don't look for it to be...
Just make the best of it –
By being the best u can be...

You

You are precious as a flower –
That dances in the sun…
Watered by the Lord –
And cleansed by His blood…
Your petals spread and bloom –
While your fragrance fills the room…
At night you're protected –
By the glow of the moon…
Your roots are embedded deep –
In Jesus who helps you grow…
Why does God love you so? –
You may never know…

You Are All I Need

Everyone compliments you –
But you're all I need…
You enjoy my company –
But you live amongst the trees…
And laugh at my jokes…
Our love is unconditional –
We'll never give it up…
You love when it rains –
Because it helps you grow…
You dance in the breeze –
Just a putting on a show…
You're arrayed in bright colors –
For all eyes to see…
You're desired by all –
But you're all I need…

A Raging Storm

As the storm rages –
My spirit is brought low…
I've pleaded for help –
Yet my prayers were ignored….
The waves of the storm –
Overflowed my shores…
In the midst of my storm –
I desire to hear God's voice…
Could it be He has spoken? –
Yet I'm afraid –
Distracted and can't focus…
As the lightning strikes –
The rain pours…
The storm rages on –
As if there is no end…
The wind is gusting –
Causing the palm trees to bend…
The beach is deserted –
I'm the only one here…
I can't hear God speak –
Because my ears are muffled by fear…
Slowly the storm moves –
Destroying everything in its path…
I'm left desolated –
Causing my conscience to be saddened…
Will I rebuild –
Or simply move on?...
This used to be my safe haven –
This used to be my home…
Storms cause destruction –
But this too shall pass…

Encouraging Word

(Isaiah 26:3)

Every morning we must awaken, determined to seek God with everything in us. When we neglect to do this, then it is that the enemy creeps in and tries his best to destroy us. Isaiah 26:3, KJV, says God will keep our mind, heart, and life in perfect peace, if we keep our mind stayed on Him.

We must always keep our focus on Jesus, because He promises to keep us in perfect peace. During our trials or storms, we must remember that God is in it with us. God is giving us His peace, protection and wisdom to get through it. It is normally during our trials and storms when we cry to God the most. No one enjoys storms, but we must understand that they help us to grow, and to draw closer to God....

A Prayer

"Lord, I know there will be storms in my life. I also know You will go through every storm with me. Lord, help me to trust You at my lowest and lonely moments in life. Help me to remember Your every promise You have made to me personally. Lord, You have given me examples of what will happen if I were to take my eyes off You.

I see what Peter did when You called him out of the boat to walk on water with You. He had the faith to get out of the boat, but he took his eyes off You. Once he did that, he began to sink. Lord, help me to stay focused on You, so I won't focus on my storm and begin to sink.

Lord, I ask You to help me to keep my eyes on You. I ask all of this in Jesus' name. Amen."

Drowning in You

I couldn't have imagined –
That drowning could be so exciting…
Till I found myself –
Drowning in your love fountain…
Being consumed by your love –
Takes my breath away…
I'm drowning with a smile –
Disregarding my desire to pray…
As I sink deeper –
Our love becomes clearer…
I never want to ascend to your surface –
So I'll make my home here…

Jesus' Return

Earth heard a yell –
And a horn blew…
The sky opened –
As Jesus came through…
Those that believed –
Smiled within their hearts…
Giving praise and worship –
To the one true God…
At His return –
His people rejoiced…
Knowing Heaven was their destination –
Because they had made the right choice…
With righteousness He judged –
Everyone who had lived…
Judging the hearts of people –
For every deed they did…
"Come," He called, –
And every righteous soul began to rise…
Those who had wrongly chosen
Had fear in their eyes…
Every knee shall bow –
And every tongue shall confess…
That Jesus is the Son of God –
Manifested in the flesh…

Can't See Pass My Past

Remembering my mistakes –
Makes me hard to believe…
You tell me how you done changed –
But you don't think…
Change can happen in me –
Selfish, unfaithful, and full of lies…
This was the reward of those –
Who allowed me in their lives…
When the heart of a man changes –
So does his ways…
He builds up and encourages –
Not takes things away…
He's a beacon of light in someone else's storm –
He's a shelter from the storm…
Before the hail comes –
With time you will see…
What you don't want to believe –
How maturity changes a man…
Into someone you can believe –
Trust is not earned…
It's something you give –
You can always be caught in your past…
Or you can let it go and live –

I Know Who I am

My place to stay –
Doesn't determine who I am…
You can call me an inmate –
But I'm still a man…
My uniform doesn't determine who I am –
I'll still be respectful…
And say, "Yes, Ma'am" and "No, Ma'am" –
You can dress me in all white…
But it won't lower my confidence –
You can try to belittle me…
But I'll just rise above it –
You can put me in a cell…
But I'll still be free –
Because I refuse to let a cell…
Dictate where I can be –
You can lock all the doors…
But I'll still come and go –
I refuse to let locked doors…
Stagnate my growth –
You can place me in a hostile environment…
But I'll still find peace –
I refuse to conform to my environment…
I'll make it conform to me –
You can take all I have…
But I'll still be blessed –
I've educated myself…
And you can never take that –

A Lighthouse in Your Storm

Lost at sea –
Being tossed by a storm…
Anchored in God's mercy –
As I desperately held on…
Blinded by the storm –
That darkens my way...
Damage may occur –
As I'm beaten by the waves…
When hope seemed all gone –
The light appeared….
God shone His light on me –
To remind me He is near…
A lighthouse –
In the midst of my storm …
God gives me light –
So I can see where I am going…
But I'll get through…
Because God gives me hope –
While encouraging me through…

Encouraging Word

(John 8:36)

So many are trapped, incarcerated and held against their will, either because of their own mistakes, or someone else's. I've learned that you don't have to be in prison or jail to be locked up. So many people are in prison in their own homes, locked in bad relationships or trapped by drugs. I can only believe that you, like millions of others, have a great desire to be free. Maybe you have tried everything, but you can't seem to free yourself. Try Jesus!! When nothing or nobody can help you, Jesus can. I'm a living example that Jesus is the only true way to freedom. Cry out to Him, and give Him permission to set you free. Whom the Son sets free…he is free indeed. Amen, Amen, Amen!

A Prayer

"Father God, I love You more than anything! I confess to You that I'm helpless without You. I've tried so hard to free myself from the bonds I'm currently held by. Although I fight to escape them, I find myself falling deeper into them. Lord, please free me!! I believe You can, and I trust You will, Lord. Every day is a battle to try to overcome myself, and everything else that exalts itself against me. I've learned that to be truly free, I must allow You to do as You choose in my life. Lord, I surrender to You. I take my hand off my life. Make Your desires mine, so I can live free in You. In Jesus' name, Amen, Amen, Amen."

When Heaven Calls

When Heaven calls –
Another saint is needed…
Heaven begins to rejoice –
As Heaven's hosts start singing…
The mercy of God –
Carries His saints home…
We appear before our Savior –
As we kneel before His throne…
When Heaven calls –
Another Angel is needed…
Heaven opens its gates –
As the hosts of Heaven start cheering…
Melody of Heaven –
Is all that we will hear…
The hosts of Heaven celebrate –
Our help is finally here…
When Heaven calls –
White doves are released…
Our spirits leave this earth –
As we enter God's peace…

Set on Seeking You

When I awaken –
My eyes and mind…
Are set on seeking You –
You're my focal point…
In all that I do –
I look to You…
For the work that must be done –
Knowing it's You…
That keeps me going –
My full attention…
You have –
I relinquish control…
So You can direct my path –
Lord, my mind and eyes…
Are set on seeking You –
I refuse to fall victim to…
What the enemy desires me to do –
I've submitted…
With my heart, mind, and soul –
I acknowledge You are God…
And it's You who are in control –

Find What You Desire in Yourself

Being hurt touches something deep within –
It can cause a person to clam up…
With hopes of never being hurt again –
Some search for love and compassion…
Because they desperately desire a companion –
Instead of letting hurt run its course…
Hurt blinds us –
Forcing us to make bad choices…
Slow down and look within yourself –
Take inventory of your life…
To see what you have left –
If it's only a little…
Then there is still hope –
You can search this world…
And still not be able to –
Replace the one you love most…
Search within yourself –
To find strength…
Learn to love yourself –
Because that is where true love begins…

Spring Has Finally Come

As spring arrives –
The winter snow begins to melt…
Nature springs up –
Once again revealing herself…
Flowers toil beneath the sun –
As birds sing and hum…
Animals running and playing –
Spring has finally come…
The grass is green –
As flowers bloom…
Streams begin to run –
Winter has come and gone…
And spring has finally come…

Remember to Smile

Always remember to smile –
Regardless of what comes your way…
Knowing your smile –
Helps others through their day…
Life here is temporary –
But in Heaven we'll stay…
So just live and laugh –
While thanking God for today…
Continue to sing and worship –
While giving God praise…
Because none of us know –
If today will be our last day…

Word of Encouragement

(Genesis 22:2)

"Then He said, "Take now your son, your only son Isaac, whom you love, and go to the land of Moriah, and offer him there as a burnt offering on one of the mountains of which I shall tell you."

Climbing a mountain can be a very difficult experience. The climb that Abraham had taken with his only son Isaac was a very important one that revealed the intent of Abraham's heart. We too will, or have already been called to make decisions that will reveal the true desire of our hearts. Obedience to the will of God is not always easy. But it builds a deeper relationship with God. It is when we are on the stretch that God is pleased and our obedience develops a Christ-like character in us of which God can be proud.

A Prayer

"Lord, sacrifices are hard to do, so please Lord, teach me to sacrifice the things You desire of me. Lord, I thank You for not withholding Your only Son who came to earth to die for me, so that I may be reunited to You. Lord, when You ask for a sacrifice and I don't desire to give it, help me to be obedient to You by doing Your will. Lord, help me!!! Give me Your strength to climb the mountains that You have for me to climb.

Lord, I desire to be able to give my all to You, my first, my last, and my heart to You! In Jesus' name, Amen, Amen, Amen!"

About God's Business

I've been going through life –
Minding my own business…
Failing on every level –
Till God gave me a vision…
He opened my eyes to life –
And I started realizing…
What was missing –
And that to get to where I need to be…
Is not always a competition –
All I truly needed was to …
Humble myself and submit –
But before I can truly see change…
I must admit –
That minding my business…
Got me nowhere –
And the place I'm supposed to be…
That God would get me there –
So I'll stay ready and focused…
While knowing as long as He is in control –
My journey isn't hopeless…
So I'll take the attention off me –
And humbly place it where it should be…
On God's business –

Just a Touch from Heaven

Just a touch from Heaven –
Could change this world…
It could open the eyes of God's children –
And give us hearts that care…
Just a touch from Heaven –
Could heal this world…
It could fill our hearts with joy –
That everyone desires to share…
Just a touch of Heaven –
Could remove all hate…
It could fuel our "Good Morning!"-
Where it is not forced, or fake…
Just a touch from Heaven –
Could change our lives….
It could be a cure for cancer –
It could heal and it can keep alive…
Just a touch –
Is all this world needs…
A touch of Your grace and mercy –
Could meet our every need…
Just a touch of Heaven –
Can remove our cares…
Just a touch from Heaven –
Will show us God is there…

Keep Going

When they say you'll fail –
Keep going…
When you get weary
Keep going…
When all odds are against you –
Keep going…
When it seems like things are not getting better –
Keep going…
When your mind says you can't
Keep going…
When everyone else gives up –
Keep going…
When your friends go astray –
Keep going…
Finally, when you meet your goal –
Keep going…
When you think you've done enough –
Keep going…
And always remember it is God who gives you strength -
To keep going…

Focused

Quitting is not an option –
And failure is not for me…
Focused and determined –
To be all that I can be…
Strength beyond my own –
To help me along the way…
Memories of my past –
Are my fuel for today…
Tuned in to who I am –
So negativity never hurts…
It only motivates me –
And shows me what I'm worth…

If Only I Could See

Can you imagine how hard –
Living blind must be…
To be surrounded by noise –
You can't see…
To wake up daily –
With hopes of a peep…
Having to be led around life –
Like a sheep…
Having only the privilege of smelling your food –
And not seeing what you eat…
What about the many nights I've cried –
Constantly questioning and asking God why…
To hear the news talking about race –
And never having the opportunity…
To see your own face –
Let alone someone else's…
How about to look into a mirror –
And not see yourself…
Yet, I'm told to be strong –
Everyone around me is having fun…
While I'm left in this darkness alone –
At times I don't want to go on…
Yet, I continue to remain strong –
I'm constantly reminded… -
I'm not in this alone –
So, I strive to make a difference…
To make this world a safer place –
For blind people to live in…
If only I could see –
I'll help those in need…
I'll admire God's beauty –
From mountain to sea…

Word of Encouragement

(1 Thessalonians 5:16-18)

As real children of God, we follow God's commandments, and because of our obedience God manifests Himself even more to us.

In 1 Thess. 5:16-18, God says we are to rejoice forevermore. God is saying that regardless of what comes our way, we are to greatly rejoice. We are to pray without ceasing for everybody and every situation. We are also told to give thanks always and in everything. We are to always give thanks for God's protection, provision, mercy, love and every other thing He does for us. In doing as He asks of us, then we should always rejoice.

Each of us should also remember to give God thanks while always rejoicing.

A Prayer

"Father God, I thank You for allowing me to see another day. I thank You for Your love, and Your grace and mercy. Lord, regardless of what my day may bring, I pray I'm still rejoicing and giving You thanks for my trials, my accomplishments, and the talent You have blessed me to have. I pray constantly that You will use this gift You have given me that I may write for Your glory!

Lord, teach me to pray without ceasing. Teach me to rejoice forever- more, and to love You wholeheartedly. Lord, bless those who are downtrodden, in pain, suffering in their bodies, dealing with mental illness, and those who are suffering for Your name's sake.

In Jesus' name, Amen!"

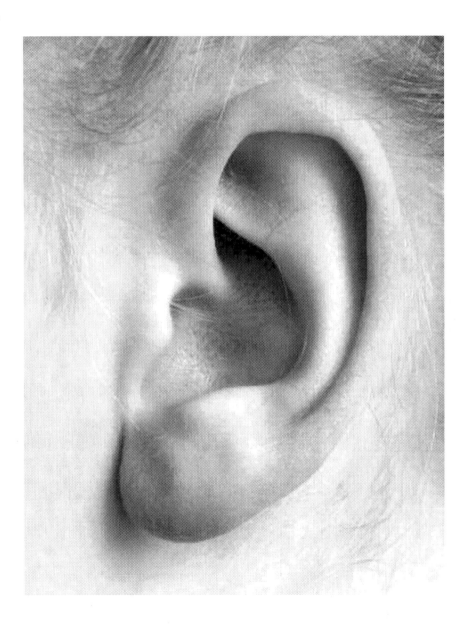

Our Hope is in Jesus

Madness all around –
As evil has its way…
God is speaking –
Yet not many care to hear…
What He has to say –
Open your ears and hear His voice…
Seek to understand His commandments –
And make your final choice…
A virus running rapidly –
Destroying everything in its path…
Whole families are being destroyed –
If they are caught in its path…
Rumors of war –
Storms like never before…
Families are in disarray –
As we draw closer to that glorious day…
Listen, people and hear God speak –
Repent of your sins…
And take heed to those who were sent –
The time to pray is now at hand…
This is a warning to God's people –
It's time to stand…
Ignoring His signs will cost us more –
Accept Jesus, and let's end this war…
Home alone with time to spare –
Draw closer to God, for He cares…
Read His word and continue to pray –
As His word comes to pass…
Before our face –
In these times of trial…
When our faith is tested –
Trust in God, all who are restless…

LOVE

Laughter, tears, they all help us grow –
Love, patience and concern is all my heart knows…

Others are affected by all we go through –
So we continue to hope in JESUS to pull us through…

Victory and success is what we seek –
Striving for excellence that all can see….

Every day on Earth is to be cherished –
Engulf yourself in God's Word…
And you will be nourished –
Because a life in Jesus is one that will flourish…

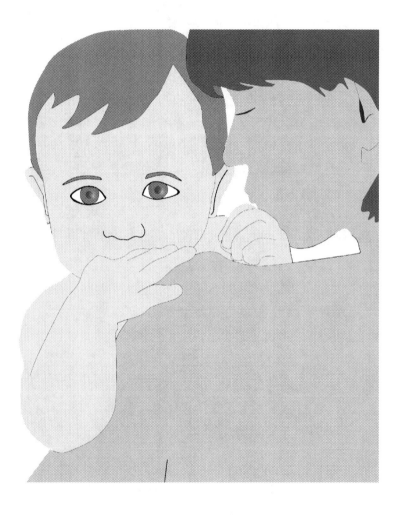

Beauty Within

Your eyes - your smile –
Are all the blind can see…
But God has gifted me –
With eyes that can truly see…
As God reveals your heart –
I'm blown away…
Of the strength you possess –
To survive another day…
Though times continue to get hard –
You continue to fight while trusting in God…
Beauty outwardly passes with time –
But beauty of one's heart…
Continues to becomes more beautiful –
Even over time…
To say you are beautiful –
Is not satisfying enough…
But to truly express your beauty in words –
It's "beautifullesiousious" which is not a word…
But this word is shared between us –

Why Me???

Jesus, why me?
My dearest child –
Who would you rather it be?...
My child, you were created for My purpose –
My child, know that it breaks My heart...
Seeing you hurting –
Sweetie, how would other young people...
Learn to stay strong? –
They will learn from your testimony...
But you must learn on your own –
Through it all, I'm by your side...
Hurt and broken –
With every tear you cry...
Be of good cheer –
You will overcome...
This will be your testimony –
For years to come...
Lives will be changed –
From hearing your story...
You will finally be free –
But it will give Me the glory...
So the next time it gets hard –
And you want to ask why...
Just remember My story –
And the reason I died...
(John 15:13-14/ I received healing Mar. 27, 2020)

Till We Meet Again

Oh, how I miss you –
In so many ways…
Just waking up for me –
Is hard these days…
Life was going good –
Then you were gone…
Gone to rest in Jesus –
Leaving me alone…
I imagine how you will smile when He calls your name –
How you will stroll into His glory…
Knowing then nothing will be the same –
No more hurt or pain…
Then with all the saints you will admire everything –
Streets paved with gold, angels singing…
When we all enter Heaven –
Heaven's bells will start ringing…
Jesus will say to you, Welcome, my child –
You have run your race…
Telling everybody who would listen –
About My saving grace…
Take your rest now; your race has been won –
Your family is fine…
I hold them in my arms –
Just take your rest, Grandma…
You have given us enough –
Everyday I'm reminded…
Of your unconditional love –
I wish your presence was with me now…
But I know God is watching me from above –
In time we will meet again…
My love, you have done your part –
You helped me receive Jesus in my heart…
I praise Him for you, EVERLINE KING –
Your memories will live on…
Yes, every one! …

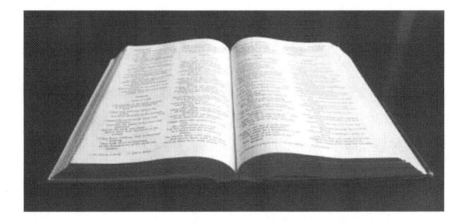

Word of Encouragement

(Psalm 100:1-5)

We are to always make a joyful noise unto the Lord. He has done so much for us as His people. He has given us the strength to still live, even as we dealt with COVID-19 and everything else. We are to serve the Lord with the right attitude in our hearts and minds. We are to do everything as if we are doing it all unto the Lord. When we do that, God gives us more strength and wisdom to truly serve Him. When we fully understand that God created us, then we realize He created us to do His work.

So let's enter God's gates with thanksgiving, and go into His courts with praise. He deserves nothing less!

A Prayer

"Lord, life has been difficult here, but regardless of how difficult it gets, You always find a way to get us through. In the middle of our loss You comfort us and lift us up, reminding us that we have a work to be done.

Lord, I do worship You, I praise you, and I pray that my serving You brings You glory. Lord, help those who are in a situation like mine, and give them the push they need to be overcomers in You. When I am down, help me to look up to You. Teach me to always worship You in spirit and in truth.

In Jesus' name, Amen!"

Missing You Like Crazy

My love for you –
Is greater than anything I've known…
The pain in my heart –
Reminds me of our song…
Remember when we first heard it? –
Remember how it moved us to tears? …
But now when I hear it –
It makes me wish you were here …
As tears threaten to come –
I'll just let them flow …
I imagine us having one last dance –
This time I'll never let you go …
How does one get past a pain so rare? –
I try to keep living, but life's not fair …
They say time heals all pain –
Yet mine remains …
I've learned to cherish every day –
I hear you telling me …
To continue to live –
But how could I??? …
When my heart won't heal!!!

Only You, Jesus

Only You, Jesus, can
Take what others
Deem unfit and
Make it desirable…
Only You can
Change the heart
Of a man – change
It from a waste -
Land – to a beautiful island… Only You were able to see me at my
lowest – The deepest struggles I had that no one else noticed… Only You
have the answers to the questions I have – How blessed I am to have an
understanding Dad… Only You could move all distractions – Though we
know You didn't cause the corona virus… but You allowed it to happen…
Only You can save –
Only You rose from the grave…
Only to You will I pray –
And only through You is
the Way…

Black Rose

As summer arrives –
We begin to grow…
Reaching toward the sun
We spread our petals…
Putting on a show –
I've always been called different…
And made fun of by my peers –
All of my siblings have found homes…
Yet I'm still here –
Families would come collect them…
As they laughed and cheered –
I'll stand up and say, "Take me"
Yet not one family did…
I'll watch summer come and go –
As I continued to grow…
Surviving the harsh winter alone –
In the freezing cold…
Every summer –
More of my siblings would grow…
Only for me to remain –
And to watch the new ones go…
A black rose –
In the midst of what people called beauty…
It's easy to become depressed –
When you're not the one they're choosing…

Giver or a Taker

Do you take? –
Or do you give? ...
You have been empowered –
With a gift to make things live…
With Love –
You make a flower bloom…
In the heart of a giver –
Taking has no room…
Those that take destroy –
Their victims beg and plead…
Only to be ignored –
Their selfish way of thinking…
Leaves a void –
God sends a giver…
To heal –
The taker flees…
And his victim lives –

Stand Together

It's our time to stand –
Not as a race, but as a man…
There is no I in us –
No doubt in trust…
You have my back –
I have yours…
Together we will face this world –
And make a difference…
For all boys and girls –
We're not afraid to face opposition…
We stay focused on our mission –
No matter what comes our way…
Hold your position –
Black – white – or brown…
Together we hold each other down –
We are a team…
With one goal in mind –
Your problems are mine…
And mine are yours –
Together let's raise our voices…
On one accord –
If you're not down with UNITY…
Your point is void! –

Word of Encouragement

There is not too much you can do that is greater than taking care of your responsibility. Every day we are to awaken determined to man up and face our responsibility with the right mindset. Life isn't going to always be fair, but it's our responsibility to continue to stay focused through it all. Always remember that your decisions do not only affect you. They affect everyone with whom you come in contact. When your way becomes tiring, trust God to help you get through everything you're facing. If you have neglected your responsibility today, then tomorrow may be too late. Take care of your duties today. You'll be happy you did.

ROMANS 12
Be joyful in hope, patient in affliction, faithful in prayer. NIV

A Prayer

"Father God, forgive me for being lazy, for continuing to dodge my responsibility, when I know that You require more out of me. Lord, You say in Your Word, that if we lack wisdom, we should ask and You will give it freely to us. Lord, give me Your wisdom today! Give me the strength and the desire to do the things I need to do. Lord, I've been neglecting my duties! Please forgive me, as I take care of them today.

I ask all this in faith!
Amen..."

Some Will and Some Won't

Some people will love you –
Some will not…
Just remember to use it as fuel –
And give life all you got…
What you say in time will pass –
But your deeds will not…
How will people remember you? –
Or would you rather they not? ...
Every day is an opportunity to right a wrong –
Your deeds done in love –
Are the words to your song…
Some may sing along –
And others may dance…
Some may hate it –
Just stick to your plan…

A Mother like You

I wish every child –
Had a mother like you…
Someone who would constantly –
Encourage her children…
In everything they go through –
Someone who pays attention…
To their accomplishments and faults –
Someone who has the wisdom to educate…
From the lessons she was taught –
I wish every child…
Had a mother like you –
Someone who is as loving…
And understanding like you –
Someone who puts her kids first…
In all that she'll do –
Someone who goes above and beyond…
To be a good mother –
Could you imagine…
How different this world would be? –
If everyone had…
You for a mother –

The Whole Armor of God

(Ephesians 6:13)

Protect yourself –
From the woes of today…
Because of the craftiness of your enemy –
As he seeks to lead you astray…
Guard your heart and mind –
With truth…
Put on the helmet of salvation –
While protecting yourself…
With the shield of faith too –
Be strong in the Lord…
And in the power of His might –
Take up the sword of the Spirit…
For it's your weapon in this fight –
Let your feet be shod…
In the preparation of peace –
Walking in God's promises…
While allowing God's Spirit to lead –
Arm yourself…
With the whole armor of God –
While staying ready for battle…
For these days are dark –

Press On

(Philippians 3:12-14)

So much comes against me –
But I refused to be moved…
I have a decision to make –
And I must live…
With the choices I choose –
So when life is unfair…
I must remember to stay the course –
Pressing toward the mark…
While remembering who this journey is for –
I Press on…
Regardless of what comes my way –
Knowing that each trial will be difficult…
That I will be faced with today –
When life says I'm nothing…
I remember who I am –
I'll continue to press on…
While I continue to stand –
So press on…
While staying focused on your task –
You have been empowered with God's strength…
To leave behind your past –
So Press On…
While keeping your eyes on your goal –
Remember it is only your destiny…
You can control–
-PRESS ON-

How I See You

Oh, how I would love –
To tell you how beautiful you are…
To compliment your inner beauty with words –
While painting a picture of your heart…
Your speech is splendid –
As you speak in design…
You walk gracefully and elegantly –
As you walk outside of time…
When you speak –
It could only be compared to an angel…
Your words capture my thoughts and attention –
It's as if it's a melody…
To a song you are singing –
To look into your eyes…
Is to admire the beauty of God's stars –
While looking in your eyes…
I'm able to see into your heart –
Inner beauty becomes beautiful…
Over a period of time –
You are as loving as a mother…
While as fierce as a lion –
Without trying you demand respect …
Your inner beauty shows –
Regardless of where you're at…
Gracefully you move –
As if floating on a cloud…
Your presence changes the mood of any room –
With just one smile…
What I'm able to see in you –
Natural eyes can't see…
I'm amazed at this discovery –
Of the woman God created you to be…

Word of Encouragement

(Mark 10:17-22)

There is a spark of divinity in the believer that it's more than works. We must have a relationship with God. The Rich Young Ruler acknowledged he did the works, but he asked Jesus what else to do, because he felt a void that works left!

When we understand who Jesus is to us, we develop an intimate relationship with Him. Who we are is revealed, and greater works He can do though us. (Matthew 16:18).

A Prayer

"Father God, I desire to truly know You as my Lord and Savior. Give me a hunger to read Your word and to search You out in Your word. I never want to get so caught up in serving that I forget to have an intimate relationship with You. Lord, let me not be like the Rich Young Ruler who refused to forsake all that he had to gain You. Today, I surrender all I have. Please use me for a vessel of honor for Your glory. Help me to glorify You in my daily walk.

I ask this in Jesus' name, Amen!"

A Beautiful Summer

Let us admire the beauty –
Of this amazing summer…
God has given us this beautiful season –
As its blue sky blankets us like covers…
The beauty of summer –
Brings together lovers…
The fish are swimming –
While the birds fly above us…
*** This summer day is like no other ***
Kids laughing and playing –
While enjoying this summer…
With their fathers and mothers –
Nature was awakened when spring arrived…
But Nature started living –
From what summer provides…
Rabbits and deer are out in droves –
Flowers and grass slow dance…
Under the summer breeze –
With roses and cloves…
Family trips are taken –
To relieve our minds…
Laughter is heard from miles away –
Parks and swimming pools are packed…
On this beautiful summer day –

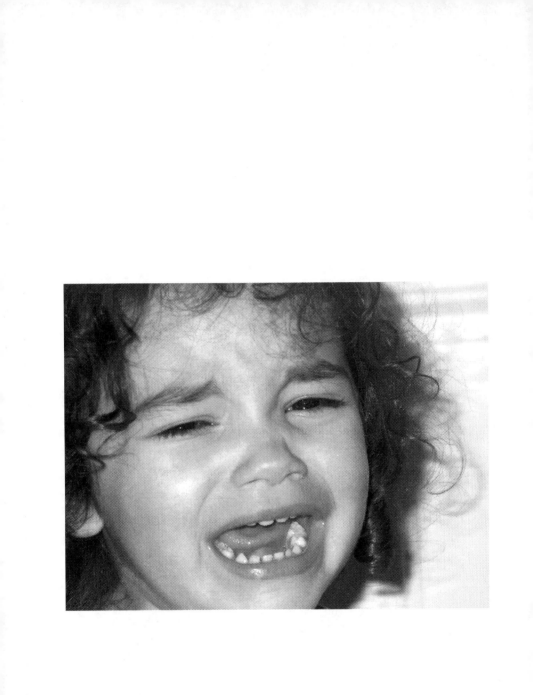

If Tomorrow Never Comes

Today has been difficult –
Nothing has gone my way…
Everything I've tried to accomplish –
Seems to backfire in my face…
Everyone seems ungrateful –
For the job that I have done…
I just wish today would pass –
So tomorrow could finally come…
Today I saw a child crying –
And there was nothing I could do…
I witnessed a four-car pileup –
That no one made it through…
I witnessed the tears of a mother –
Heartbroken for her child…
I'm ready for this day to end –
So tomorrow can begin…
But if tomorrow never comes –
Lord, just help us on this day…
We bow our hearts before You –
We humble ourselves and pray…

Beneath the Surface

Deep beneath the ocean's surface –
Lives a world most have yet to see…
Droves of exotic fish –
And colorful coral reefs…
Killer whales and great white sharks –
Patrolling the ocean's deep…
Bottom dwellers searching the ocean's floor –
Looking for something to eat…
Surfers surfing –
Riding the ocean's waves…
A variety of animals –
Dwelling in ocean caves…
Beneath the ocean's surface –
What a sight for eyes to see! …
Though many admire the ocean's surface –
Its beauty lies beneath…

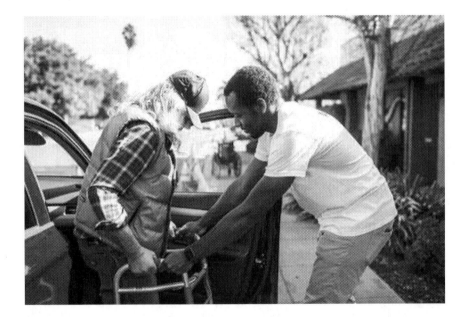

What Kindness is

Kindness is love in action –
Love demands forgiveness…
Regardless to what has happened –
Kindness highlights other people's needs…
In a heart filled with kindness –
It inspires others to breathe…
Kindness breeds gentleness –
It motivates you to be sensitive and forgiving…
Kindness encourages one to be willing –
Willing to comfort others…
Regardless of how you're feeling –
Kindness attracts lovers…
It's an act of second nature –
Shown by mothers…
What kindness truly is –
It is simply loving others…
OH yeah!!! –
It's a gem desiring to be discovered…
That's what kindness is -

They Gave Their All

Today we salute our soldiers –
Who gave their all…
Marching on the front line –
While answering our nation's call…
As our flag flies high –
We salute it with pride…
Knowing each time we salute –
We salute to our veterans…
Even our veterans who have died –
Bravely each of y'all…
Laced up y'all boots –
Kissed loved ones and said "Goodbye"
Not knowing if it was the last thing y'all would do …
Made promises that you would return –
Gifted with the opportunity to travel…
We could only imagine the things y'all learned –
Late night walks looking for trip wires…
Bombs bursting, lighting up the night sky –
No words are heard as they sat there and cried…
In the barracks bonds were formed –
Men and women soldiers…
Wearing camo and armed –
Determined to protect their fellow soldiers…
Some with their kids' pictures tucked away in their pocket –
As if they could hold 'em…
We salute you on this Memorial Day –
America is still free…
Because y'all made sure it stayed that way –
Happy Memorial Day!

Word of Encouragement

(Ephesians 5:28)

Husbands, you are to love your wives, as God demanded you to do. We are to live peacefully with our wives, while encouraging them to be the best they can be. Husbands, you must be the example to your wives, kids and others, while walking in the commandments of God.

Wives, help teach your husbands how to love, and always cherish you and y'all family. There must be an open and clear line of communication for y'all's relationship to work.

Children, love your parents, cherish them and always respect them, because this is pleasing to God.

A Prayer

"Heavenly Father, today I pray for all families. I pray that the husband, who is the head of the family, is living according to Your standards. Give us men the desire and hunger to lead by Your examples. Lord, we need You today, to keep us submitted to You, so we can always do according to Your will in our daily lives. Help us, Lord, to be the men You have created us to be. Help us to cherish, love, provide for and protect our families always.

In Jesus' name.... Amen!"

Poems for Cards

Happy Anniversary!

Another year with the one I love
Many memories -
Shared between us …
Happy Anniversary -
And many more …
Another year is past -
For the both of us …
Happy Anniversary!

I Miss You!

When I think of you -
My heart skips a beat …
Oh, how I long -
For the next time we meet …
Thinking of you!

You & I

Loving you endlessly –
With a heart that overflows…
Watering our love with deeds –
As it continually grows…
Love you!

Poems for Cards

Momma

You are rare –
You are loved…
There is nothing to compare –
With my mother's love…
Happy Mother's Day!

Daddy

You are strict –
You are fair…
You've been my example –
You show me you care…
Happy Father's Day!

A Special Birthday

Laugh –
Cry…
Enjoy your day –
Invite some friends over…
And celebrate –
Happy Birthday!

A Wolf in Sheep's Clothing

Dressed in a disguise –
So you can't see who I am…
Pretending to be your brother –
A son of I AM…
My ways are deceptive –
As I distract you from the truth…
A wolf in sheep's clothing –
Pretending to be like you…
I twist the truth –
To lead you astray…
I'm deceiving and deceptive –
Even when we pray…
The father of all liars –
I'm poisonous as a snake…
I'm a false prophet –
Preaching against faith…
A wolf in sheep's clothing –
Who lives amongst believers…
Scheming and plotting –
To turn you from Jesus…

Poems for Your Soul

This book was written to share my life journey, with you in mind. Not every poem is about me, but somehow, some way, something brought me to the point where each of these poems had to be written. I hope as you read this book, you are encouraged and motivated. I pray that it will give you the desire to share your heart as well.

There are so many people I want to thank for helping to make **"Poems for Your Soul"** come true. I first want to thank my Lord and Savior Jesus Christ, because without Him, I wouldn't have a heart that speaks to me and others. I want to thank my grandmother, Everline King, who has been my everything. R.I.P., my love! I thank my mother Barbara King, my Uncle Ricky, and my everything Lesley H. King. There are so many more folks who had to listen to me read my new poems every day. There are a chosen few, who always showed me what I could have done better, and I'd like to thank all of you. It's because of you that this book has life!

Poems for Your Soul II is already in the works. Enjoy! ☺

By Cenca King (LP)